Supervisor's Guide To

Documenting Employee Discipline

Fourth Edition

by

Lee Paterson
Attorney at Law
Sonnenschein Nath & Rosenthal
Los Angeles, California

Mike Deblieux
President
Mike Deblieux Human Resources
Tustin, California

LEXIS® Law Publishing
Parker Publications, Inc.
Carlsbad, CA

Fourth Edition Published 1998
Printed and bound in the United States of America

ISBN: 0-327-00884-9

8244711

TABLE OF CONTENTS

ABOUT THE AUTHORS v

CHAPTER 1: INTRODUCTION 1
- Effective Documentation 2
- Document Before Taking Action 3
- Critical Incidents Diary 3
- Keeping Documentation 6

CHAPTER 2: WRITING DOCUMENTATION 9
- FOSA+ Step 1: Facts 9
  1. Employee Behavior 9
  2. Third-Party Observations 12
  3. Employee Interview 13
- FOSA+ Step 2: Objectives 16
- FOSA+ Step 3: Solutions 19
- FOSA+ Step 4: Action 20

CHAPTER 3: REASONS FOR DISCIPLINE 23
- Reduction in Force (Layoff) 23
- Violation of Company Rules 23
- Inability to Perform 26

CHAPTER 4: SUMMARY 29
- FOSA+ Step 1: Facts 29
- FOSA+ Step 2: Objectives 29
- FOSA+ Step 3: Solutions 30
- FOSA+ Step 4: Action 30

DISCIPLINE FLOWCHART 31

CHECKLIST BEFORE DISCIPLINE 32

INCIDENT INVESTIGATION REPORT 33

SAMPLE DOCUMENTATION 35
1. Performance Objectives Memo 37
2. Counseling Memo 41
3. Memorandum of Oral Warning—Poor Work Performance 43
4. Memorandum of Oral Warning—Violation of Work Rule 45
5. Written Warning—Poor Work Performance 47
6. Written Warning—Violation of Work Rule 51
7. Suspension Notice—Poor Work Performance 53
8. Suspension Notice—Violation of Work Rule 57
9. Probation Notice—Poor Work Performance 59
10. Probation Notice—Violation of Work Rule 61
11. Day of Contemplation Memo—Violation of Work Rule 63
12. Last Chance Agreement—Violation of Work Rule 65
13. Termination Notice—Poor Work Performance 67
14. Termination Notice—Violation of Work Rule 69

INDEX 71

ABOUT THE AUTHORS

Lee Paterson is an employment law attorney in the firm of Sonnenschein Nath & Rosenthal. He is past chair of the Los Angeles Area Chamber of Commerce Personnel Management Committee and is General Counsel for both PIHRA — The Professionals in Human Resources Association, the California State Council of the Society for Human Resources Management and Area VI of the Society for Human Resource Management. He is also a member of the labor relations section and management member of the Committee on Practice and Policy of the American Bar Association. His articles on arbitration, union organizing, and unfair labor practices have been published in legal reviews and trade journals. He has published a number of books on labor relations for management.

Mr. Paterson represents management exclusively in problems relating to the employer-employee relationship, including employee benefits; collective bargaining agreement negotiations; equal employment; and matters concerning employers, unions, and employees. He handles labor cases at all levels of both state and federal courts as well as cases before the National Labor Relations Board, the Department of Labor, the Equal Employment Opportunity Commission, and applicable state administrative agencies. He is also a nationally recognized speaker and regularly addresses employer groups and associations throughout the United States.

Mike Deblieux is President of Mike Deblieux Human Resources. He is a nationally recognized human resources management trainer and consultant. He presents training programs on human resource related issues such as Documenting Discipline, Writing Performance Reviews, Interviewing, Preventing Sexual Harassment, and Understanding Equal Employment Opportunity. Mr. Deblieux provides a full range of human resource consulting services to a wide variety of organizations. He writes and updates employee handbooks and personnel policy manuals.

Mr. Deblieux is an Instructor for the University of California, Irvine Extension Human Resources Management Certificate Program. He has been awarded the Extension' Distinguished Instructor Award. He is a Course Leader and a Blue Ribbon Speaker for the American Management Association (AMA), The Employer's Group and PIHRA — The Professionals in Human Resources Association. He presents over 100 programs each year to a variety of private, public, regional, state, and local organizations. He may be reached at 714-669-0309.

Lee Paterson and Mike Deblieux have written three books, *Documenting Employee Discipline*, *Supervisor's Guide to Documenting Discipline* and *Supervisor's Guide to Performance Reviews*. Their books are available from LEXIS® Law Publishing; to order, call: 1-800-542-0957. Mr. Paterson and Mr. Deblieux write monthly columns for the PIHRAScope. Their articles can be viewed each month at www.phira.org on the World Wide Web.

1
INTRODUCTION

Your primary job as a supervisor is to help people succeed at the work they perform. To get employees to succeed, you must define and explain performance expectations; acknowledge and celebrate successful performance; identify performance problems and decide what needs to be done to correct them.

One of your communication tools is the written word. You write memos, letters, and performance reviews to and about employees. Your written communication must be clear, accurate, and timely. When an employee has a performance problem, your documentation may be the tool that helps the employee to see the mistake and change a problem behavior.

In one case, a company thought an employee had been sleeping on the job, but couldn't prove it. The employee was transferred to a new supervisor, who met with the employee and went over each step of the employee's job. The supervisor went over the work rules and also told the employee what the rewards were for good work. After the meeting, the supervisor sent the employee a memo outlining the major points of their discussion. Six months later, the supervisor evaluated the employee as the best worker in the department. When the supervisor met with the employee to discuss the performance review, he asked the employee why he had not done as well in other departments. The employee answered, "Because you are the first supervisor around here to tell me exactly what you expected me to do." Your success as a supervisor depends on your ability to carefully explain, in person and in writing, what you expect of your employees.

A secondary benefit of documentation is that it protects the supervisor and the company against lawsuits. As the number and cost of employee lawsuits increase, companies are becoming more critical of supervisors who discipline employees without proper documentation. Supervisors are no longer able to "get by" without employee documentation. Your ability to handle and document employee problems is a key factor in your job performance.

It is not unusual to hear about lawsuits where companies have spent thousands of dollars defending decisions made by supervisors. In addition, in several recent employee cases, the courts have found the supervisor personally liable to the employee. In some of these cases, the court required the supervisor to pay monetary damages directly to an ex-employee. Many of these supervisors could have avoided liability by properly documenting the employee behavior that led to the termination.

Effective Documentation

Objectivity is the first step of effective documentation. You must handle performance, discipline, and termination cases as business issues. Effective business decisions and effective documentation are based on an objective analysis of factual information. Your analysis must consider all available information. It must be free of emotion and bias. It must be complete before you take any disciplinary action.

When an employee's performance is not successful, you must be able to demonstrate through your efforts and your documentation that you were an effective coach. Your documentation must allow the reader (e.g., your manager, the employee, a court, etc.) to conclude:

4. the employee has violated a company rule or failed to perform his/her job properly; and
2. you have been a supportive supervisor who made a sincere effort to help the employee succeed.

We wrote this book to help you write effective documentation. This book focuses on how to document discipline. If you use the ideas described in this book, you will be successful in documenting employee discipline, performance, and dismissal issues. Our companion book, *Supervisor's Guide to Employee Performance Reviews*, shows you how to plan, write, and present effective performance reviews. We would enjoy hearing from you after you read this book. We can be reached at 714-669-0309.

Document Before Taking Action

Discipline is a formal action against an employee. It is a serious matter which requires you to be timely, objective, and fair. You must collect accurate information and write effective documentation on employee behavior before you discipline an employee.

In a recent case, a supervisor wanted to terminate an employee for poor job performance. The supervisor had been concerned about the employee's performance for at least two years. The supervisor called human resources for advice on how to terminate the employee. She explained that the employee had, for the third time in the last year, failed to complete an important project on time. When projects were late, the customer received a discount. Because of the employee's mistakes, the company lost money. The human resources manager asked the supervisor if he had counseled the employee and documented the counseling sessions when projects were not completed on time. The supervisor responded that she talked to the employee almost daily. When the human resources manager asked for written documentation of those discussions, the supervisor didn't have any.

They pulled the employee's personnel file and found a performance review for each of the past three years. Each evaluation rated the employee as "satisfactory." The human resources manager pointed out that the company's only written proof of the employee's job performance showed that the employee was satisfactory. If the employee sued, he could deny the counseling sessions and make the supervisor look unfair and inconsistent for firing a "satisfactory" employee.

Critical Incidents Diary

You should keep a running record of each significant conversation you have with an employee. It is unnecessary to document the whole conversation; a brief summary is sufficient. A Critical Incidents Diary is an effective method for keeping track of both employee and supervisory actions. You should use your critical incidents diary to list significant events that occur with your employees.

A critical incidents diary is a reminder of an event. It is a memory jogger. It tells you what happened and when it happened. If an employee's behavior deteriorates, you can use your critical incidents diary to explain what you did to try to help the employee correct the problem. Your notes will allow you to write a clear and effective counseling memo, performance evaluation, or warning notice.

A critical incidents diary is a habit you must develop and practice. For most supervisors, a pocket or desk calendar is an excellent place to note significant employee events. It is essential for you to create an easy-to-use system that you will use consistently. Your system must clearly identify the event (e.g., who, what, when, where, how). Exhibit 1 is an example of one supervisor's critical incidents diary. Notice that the information is short and cryptic; just enough to refresh your memory, but not so long that you will put off doing it when a significant event occurs.

Exhibit 1

Critical Incidents Diary	**Week of 3/21**
Monday, March 21 9:00 A.M. Counseled John re: absenteeism	Tuesday, March 22 8:00 A.M. Frank: attended new employee orientation; signed for employee handbook
Wednesday, March 23	Thursday, March 24 10:15 A.M. Susan: oral warning — five mistakes on quarterly report
Friday, March 25 3:30 P.M. Jane: compliment from Jason, Inc. re: marketing presentation	Saturday, March 26 Sunday, March 27

Your critical incidents diary must record the following types of events:

a. Positive performance. You should make a note when an employee meets or exceeds a significant performance expectation. Recording positive information will help you to write effective performance reviews. Your notes will help you give the employee specific examples of successful performance. For example:

> January 15: Jones & Company called. Said Bill saved an order for us through after sale follow-up. Thanked Bill for a good job.

b. Performance objectives. You need to make a note in your critical incidents diary when you explain an important job, work assignment, or responsibility to an employee. Your note should indicate that on a certain date you explained a performance objective or a set of objectives for the employee to meet.

> February 20: Met with Kay. Explained the company procedures for cash control. Told her she must follow company procedures.

c. Training. You should note employee training, including personal instruction and on the job training. Your note should include information about who did the training and what the subject of the training was.

> September 28: Showed J.V. how to operate drill press. Made K.L. available to answer further questions.

d. Investigations. When you investigate a minor incident, you should put a note in your critical incidents diary to help you remember whom you talked to and what was said. For major events, of course, you will need to write a memo to explain your findings.

> February 29: Asked Mary who took crane out of the yard. She said she saw Alison Owen drive away in it at 7:00 A.M.

e. Counseling. You must note counseling as it occurs. Counseling is informal. It demonstrates you are working with the employee to correct problems at the early stages of an issue. If the employee does not correct the problem, it will be important for you to demonstrate that you began working with the employee at the earliest stages. If you do not make notes at the time the counseling is offered, it will be difficult, if not impossible, to go back and remember dates and times at a later date.

> March 3: Joan late 10 minutes. Reminded her of company tardiness rule. She said she would not be late again.

f. Oral warnings. An oral warning is the first step of formal discipline. An oral warning occurs when an employee is counseled and told further repetition of the behavior will result in discipline. If an event is serious enough to warn an employee, then it is serious enough to be documented.

> May 31: Met with Frieda. Told her that racial jokes are not tolerated in this company and any future jokes will result in discipline.

g. Progressive discipline. Each step of progressive discipline (e.g., oral warning, written warning, last step option, termination) should be recorded in your critical incidents diary. Even though such actions are documented in memo or letter form, it is important to make a note in your critical incidents diary to be sure your record is complete.

> July 5: Gave Jack three days off for taking company property home without permission.

Keeping Documentation

Your critical incidents diary is an ongoing, up-to-date record of your efforts to help employees succeed. If an employee is unsuccessful, your critical incidents diary will help show that you did your job as an effective supervisor. In case of a lawsuit, your decision to discipline or terminate an employee will probably not get to a judge or jury for three to five years. This means you must write down all important events and store all your notes in a safe place. Many termination lawsuits are lost because the supervisor cannot find the documentation and, therefore, is unable to prove an employee violated a rule or performed poorly. In the courtroom, it is essential that you have accurate and complete documentation to support your decisions. If you cannot support your testimony with clear, accurate documentation, your company and quite possibly, you personally, will very likely spend significant sums on attorney, court, and settlement costs.

2
WRITING DOCUMENTATION

One of the most important parts of documenting employee behavior is to follow a consistent format. Your documentation of employee behavior can be outlined in five basic elements. We have developed an acronym to help you remember these elements. It is called FOSA+ which stands for FACTS, OBJECTIVES, SOLUTIONS, ACTION. The + is your attitude and approach to addressing employee behavior problems.

FOSA+ Step 1: Facts

Facts are the key to effective documentation. There are five types of facts that you should look for and document.

1. Employee behavior

Employee behavior is always the most important fact leading to discipline. You must describe this behavior objectively. If you use emotions or conclusions to describe the employee's behavior, you significantly reduce the chances of the employee correcting the problem while increasing the chances of your company losing a lawsuit.

You can describe employee behavior factually by stating:

What happened,
When it happened,
Where it happened,
Who was involved,
How it happened.

Describing this information gives the employee, your manager, and any outside reviewer a clear picture of why you are concerned about the employee's behavior. It allows you to objectively document that the employee has not lived up to your expectations.

Unfortunately, we often fail to describe employee behavior by using facts. Instead, we record our subjective thoughts and assumptions. You make a subjective statement when you say things like, "He was drunk," or "She was sick again," or "He has a bad attitude." Such statements are conclusions. They will not stand up to scrutiny unless objective facts are provided to support them. Subjective statements place the employee on the defensive and reduce the likelihood that he or she will respond to your coaching. Discipline based on such statements will expose you to needless legal liability and costs.

If you want to successfully document employee behavior, you must describe your direct observations of the employee's behavior or record direct observations of others. An excellent way to do this is to use words that describe your five senses:

I saw...
I heard...
I touched...
I smelled...
I tasted...

Such statements are factual. They simply report your observations. If your statement is factual, then it will support your conclusions. For instance:

> John, I saw you report to your work station at 8:10 A.M. You are scheduled to report to work at 8:00 A.M. I heard you tell Jane Smith that you overslept because your alarm clock didn't go off.

When you read this statement, you conclude the employee was ten minutes late because he failed to check his alarm clock.

Similarly, when you describe observations made by others, you have to describe their observations in behavioral terms. For instance:

They told me they saw you...
He said he heard you...
Another employee saw you touch...
He said he tasted...
She said she smelled...

Following are some examples that will help you understand the value of documenting employee behavior factually:

Subjective Evaluation	**Objective Observation**
"You were late."	"I saw you report to your desk at 8:35 A.M." (Sight)
"You are a thief."	"I heard you tell Fred that you took the money." (Hearing)
"You didn't clean the walls."	"When I ran my hands over the walls, I could feel the oil." (Touch)
"The linens were not washed right."	"When I smelled the new laundry, it smelled sour." (Smell)
"You were drinking on the job."	"I saw you drink from the glass on your desk and I tasted the liquid in it. It tasted like vodka." (Taste)

If a subjective evaluation is necessary, it should be "objectified" by adding the observations or facts from which the evaluation is based. For example:

Subjective Evaluation	Objective Observation
"You are hostile."	"On February 1, March 3, and March 28 you used the words 'damn you' and 'go to hell' to other employees in front of customers. When I discussed this with you on March 29, you told me that it was none of my business and that I had no right to tell you what words to use. Your hostility toward customers and supervision (subjective) is not acceptable behavior in this company."
"You were drunk."	"You were under the influence of liquor (subjective). Your speech was slurred, your eyes were bloodshot, and your breath smelled strongly of liquor."
"You are a poor salesperson."	"You are performing poorly (subjective). In March you sold \$500,000. Your volume was 40% below department average and 25% below minimum standard. In January we agreed that your goal for the first six months of the year would be \$5 million. You are now 90% behind your goal."

2. Third-party observations

Third parties are more credible than either an employee or a supervisor. If there was another observer to an incident, you should get a signed statement from that person. If a signed statement is not practical, then you should have a trusted witness present when the third party tells his story.

When another person describes an employee's behavior, you should ask questions to help the person use objective observations to describe what they saw, heard, felt, tasted, and touched.

In a recent case, a supervisor was told that an employee was dealing drugs on the job. The employee who told the supervisor was his oldest and most valued friend. The supervisor acted on the information and fired the accused employee. The ex-employee sued. When the case came to trial, the supervisor went to his friend and asked her to testify. The friend refused to testify because she was afraid that her family would be attacked by a drug gang. She told the supervisor that if she was called to testify she would deny everything.

Obviously, the supervisor was left out on a limb alone with the ex-employee sawing off the branch. Before he took the action, the supervisor should have obtained a written statement from his friend detailing exactly everything she knew. He should have also tried to get statements from other employees. If he had documented his information before he took action, he would not have had a problem. Exhibit 2 is an example of a witness statement.

In addition to witness statements, you should also collect any other reports or records that exist. For example, accident reports, police reports, computer records, time cards, and other such documents can help you to explain what happened. You should ask yourself whether you need to take photographs, videotapes, or make a drawing of the incident.

3. Employee interview

You should never make a final decision about whether an employee is wrong without first giving the employee a chance to explain his or her side of the story. Even when the employee is wrong, he or she is entitled to an opportunity to explain their actions before you make a final decision. As an effective supervisor, you must demonstrate through your actions and your words that you have dealt with the employee fairly.

Exhibit 2

November 21, 2005

Los Angeles

My name is Brenda Johnson. My home address is 254 Macmillan Avenue, Ramona, California. My phone number is 619-555-6513.

On Monday, November 20, 2005, at about 10:00 A.M., I was standing in the coffee room. I was facing the north door to the room. The door was closed. Ted Jones came into the room. He was holding a stapler in his right hand. It was brown and looked just like the company stapler that I have on my desk.

I saw him hand the stapler to George Danchuck, the Office Assistant. George took the stapler from Ted and placed it in a plain cardboard box that was sitting on the floor.

I then left the coffee room.

I have reviewed this statement on the date indicated below and swear to the best of my recollection under penalty of perjury that it is true.

________________________________ _______________

Brenda Johnson, Assistant Vice President Date

Sometimes giving an employee a chance to explain can save the company from serious liability. In one case, an employee brought a gun into the plant. The supervisor wanted to fire him. After the police took the gun away from the employee, the supervisor met with him and asked him if he knew it was a violation of company rules to have a gun in the plant. The employee admitted he knew the rule! The supervisor asked him if there was a reason he had the gun. The employee said he was protecting himself because a co-worker had threatened to kill him! When the supervisor investigated, he found that it was true. If he hadn't asked, the supervisor wouldn't have known about the co-worker's threat until the lawsuit was filed.

Sometimes meeting with the employee can protect the company from serious embarrassment. In one case, a supervisor believed an employee was embezzling bank bonds. The supervisor wanted to fire the employee immediately. However, he agreed to meet with the employee. He told the employee he had questions about his record keeping and asked the employee to take him through the books. The employee broke down and confessed to stealing hundreds of thousands of dollars in customer funds. Based upon the employee's written confession, the company was able to replace the missing funds without embarrassment with its customers. If the employee had been fired, it would have had to go through an expensive and time-consuming public audit that would have ruined the company's reputation as a well-run organization.

If an employee is confronted with behavior known to you, he or she either has to admit it and explain it, or deny it. In either event, the employee has committed to one final version of what he or she did. If the employee tells the truth, it is a first step in changing his or her behavior. If the employee lies to you, and you have the facts to show it, it resolves any doubt that the employee should be disciplined.

When you interview an employee about an incident or performance issue, you should:

- Have a silent witness present who will not participate in the conversation but who will write notes down after the meeting about everything that occurred.
- Tell the employee that you are conducting an investigation. Tell the employee the general facts related to the case. Ask the employee what he or she knows about it.
- Don't accuse the employee of anything.
- Ask nonconfrontational questions such as: "Have you heard anything about the television that was taken last Friday?" "Are you aware of any problems with employee's falsifying timecards?"
- Ask open-ended questions related to the investigation such as: "Are you aware of anyone violating company policy since you started here?" or "Have you seen or heard about any incidents that you would consider sexual harassment in your department?"

- Make sure the employee's questions are answered: "Are there any questions you would like to ask?"
- If the employee asks if he is being accused tell him: "We are conducting an investigation, I haven't made up my mind about anything. I want to get all the facts before I make up my mind."
- Close the meeting with a wide-open question: "Is there anything else that you think the company needs to know that you haven't told me?"

FOSA+ Step 2: Objectives

The second step in the FOSA+ system, Objectives, involves telling the employee what is expected on the job. Once the facts of a rule violation or performance problem are known, it is your responsibility to explain to the employee how you want his or her behavior to change. It is often a good idea to get the employee involved in deciding what needs to be done to correct the problem. However, ultimately, it is your responsibility to decide what the employee must do to meet or exceed your expectations.

Supervisors frequently assume that employees know, or should know, what to do on the job, but unless employees are told what is expected, they cannot be held responsible. However, even if the employee does know what is expected, you can't prove it without documentation. Thus, if you want your disciplinary action to be successful, you must be able to document that the employee knew exactly what you wanted him or her to do. Each time you correct the employee's behavior, make a record in your critical incidents diary of what you told him or her.

When you correct the employee's behavior, you must either:

1. give the employee a specific behavior pattern to follow; or,
2. set a specific result for the employee to achieve.

Examples may include:

Specific Behavior

You use the word processor program, and type the memo exactly as it is written.

Specific Result

You must sell five copy machines per month.

Subjective (nonmeasurable) objectives allow the employee to use your unclear expectations as a defense against having to change his or her behavior. We had a case where a supervisor told an employee he had been late six times in the previous month and would have to "*improve his attendance*." The next month the supervisor fired the employee for being late 11 times in a two-month period. The employee defended himself by saying that he had only been late five times in the second month (as opposed to six instances the previous month), and he had improved! Clearly, the employee was trying to take advantage of the supervisor's subjective statement; however, the supervisor erred in giving him the opportunity.

When you write an objective, you must be sure that it is specific, positive, and explained as a requirement. A specific objective clearly defines the task or result the employee must accomplish. For example:

Incorrect: "Do a better job next time." (This is a very general objective. It cannot be objectively measured.)

Correct: "Greet each customer with a smile. Always start the conversation by saying, 'Good morning (afternoon, evening), my name is Shianne Park, how may I help you.'"

A positive objective tells the employee what to do. For example:

Incorrect: "Don't forget to wear your safety glasses next time." (This is a negative objective. It tells the employee what he or she should not do.)

Correct: "The company safety rule requires you to wear safety glasses at all times in the plant. I expect you to put your safety glasses on before you enter the manufacturing area."

A required objective makes it clear to the employee that he or she must do what you are telling them to do. For example:

Incorrect: "It would be helpful if you would check your work." (This statement allows the employee to decide whether or not to check the work. If the employee does not check his or her work, you cannot hold them accountable.)

Correct: "You must check your work before you turn it in. You must be sure that your base numbers are correct and that all math is computed correctly."

Here are some examples of specific issues and accompanying documentation that avoid subjective statements:

Issue	Documentation
Attendance	"In the future, I expect you to be at work and ready to begin working at 8:00 a.m. each day that you are scheduled to work."
Honesty	"When I ask you for information about company business, I expect you to tell me what you know at the time that I ask for the information."
Deadlines	"In the future, I expect you to complete your monthly status report by the first workday of each month."
Reports	"Your reports must include an analysis of the customer's equipment problems, the reasons for the breakdowns, the steps you have taken to correct the problems, and your recommendations for future action."
Communication	"In the future, I expect you to tell me when the computer is broken down. I expect you to tell

	me about the problem within one-half hour after you become aware of it. If I am not available, I expect you to tell Bob Andreini or Lauren Griffin."
Quality	"Your reject rate must be reduced to less than ten parts per 1,000 by January 10, and to less than five parts per 1,000 by March 1."
Cleanliness	"You must maintain a clean work environment. This means that you must clean up any liquid or powder spills immediately. It means that you must sweep your work area floor at the beginning of your shift and between 1:00 P.M. and 2:00 P.M. each day."

FOSA+ Step 3: Solutions

The third step in FOSA+ is to offer Solutions that, if used, will help the employee meet the objectives you have established. Giving an employee solutions to improve his or her behavior is one of the most important steps you can take to help the employee change behavior. In addition, if you can show that you offered the employee help to correct his or her behavior, you eliminate the suspicion that you were out to get the employee by trying to build a case against him or her. Documenting that you gave the employee solutions to help improve performance will increase your credibility with your manager and outsiders such as judges, juries, and administrative agency investigators.

The solutions you offer do not have to be elaborate. If you have an employee who has problems performing the job, you can suggest that the employee take a related course or workshop. If you have an employee who has violated a rule, you can suggest the employee re-read the rule and ask questions to help him or her understand it.

Here are a few examples of solutions that may be included in disciplinary documentation:

Solution	**Documenation**
Coaching	"I will work with you on the next project so that you will learn how to do it."
Training	"I suggest you take an accounting course at a local college."
Resource Persons	"If you have questions about the documents assigned to you, you may ask Joan to help you or review your work before you turn it in."
Resource Materials	"I am sending you a book for our spreadsheet software. It might help you to read it. The index provides a quick reference for finding answers to questions you might have about building financial models."

FOSA+ Step 4: Action

The fourth step in FOSA+ is to document the Action that you intend to take if the employee does not meet your objectives. If an incident is serious enough to bring to an employee's attention, then you need to let the employee know two things:

1. what action you are taking now; and
2. what action will occur if the employee's behavior does not change.

For example, if you are counseling the employee, you must explain that you are counseling the employee and that you will meet with him or her again in the future to discuss his or her performance. On the other hand, if you are giving the employee a warning notice, then you must explain that he or she is receiving a warning notice and that if the problem is not corrected, it will lead to further discipline up to and including termination.

Here are some sample actions for you to consider:

Event	**Action**
Training	"I will follow up with you tomorrow to see how you performed."
Counseling	"I will meet with you in thirty days to see if your attendance has improved."
Oral Warning	"This is an oral warning. If your behavior does not improve, it will result in further disciplinary action."
Written Warning	"I am giving you a written warning that will be placed in your personnel file. If you do not meet the objectives I have outlined, you will be subject to serious discipline."
Last Step Option (Suspension without pay)	"You will be suspended for three days without pay beginning Tuesday, May 12. This suspension notice will be placed in your personnel file. If you do not meet the objectives I have stated above, you will be subject to serious discipline up to and including termination."
Termination	"You are terminated effective immediately."

FOSA+ FLOWCHART

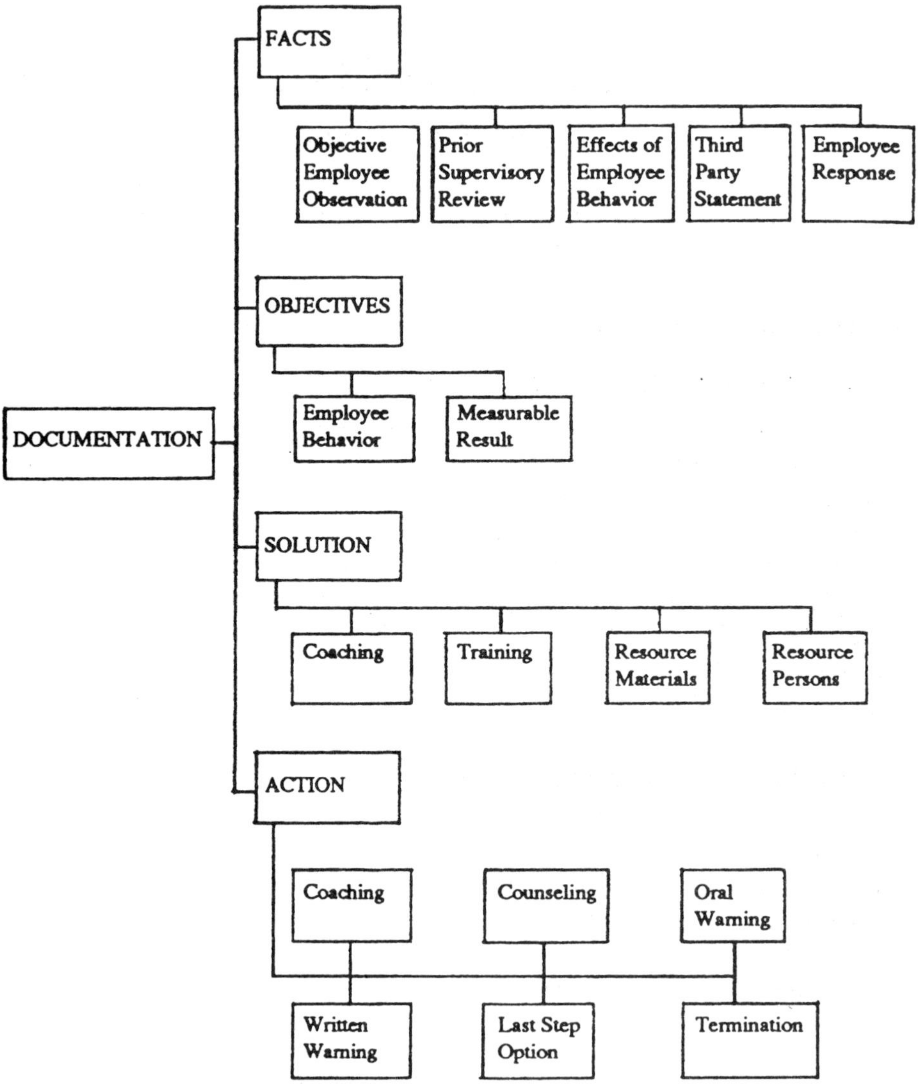

3
REASONS FOR DISCIPLINE

There are three objective reasons an employee can be terminated; only two of these are grounds for discipline.

Reduction in Force (Layoff)

You can lay off an employee whenever there has been a change in the technology of the job, when the job no longer exists, or when the job has been combined so that only one employee can perform it. Some companies call this a reduction in force. Since this is not discipline, you only have to document that there was a legitimate change in the operation of the business and that there was an objective criteria through which the laid off employees were selected (e.g., performance, prior discipline, seniority, etc.). A layoff is not a disciplinary action. It should not be used in place of discipline to terminate an employee who has violated company rules or performed poorly.

Violation of Company Rules

Documented violation of company rules or policies is a valid, objective reason for employee discipline. Tardiness, absenteeism, theft, and falsification of company records are all examples of company rule violations.

In a violation of rules case, you must show five things:

a. Rule

Employees cannot be disciplined for a rule that does not exist. Before you discipline an employee, you need to identify the specific company rule you intend to enforce. The rule must apply to the situation. For example, a rule against drinking on company premises does not include a beer in a restaurant across the street.

There are a few offenses that may not require specific written rules (e.g., criminal activity on the job, fighting, and gross insubordination). However, before disciplining without a rule, you should get advice from higher level managers, human resources professionals, and/or legal counsel.

b. Proof employee knew the rule

You have to document that the employee knew or should have known the rule. The easiest way to do that is to show that the employee was given a copy of the rules and signed a receipt for them. In addition, you should develop a habit of routinely reminding employees about company rules. An easy way to do this is to include a review of one rule at each staff meeting. When you remind employees about rules, you should make a note in your critical incidents diary.

c. Proven violation of the rule

You must document a violation of the rule before you can discipline an employee. If you observed the violation yourself, then you should write down your observation before taking any action. If there are company records or if you can create records such as drawings, photographs, etc., these should also be collected before you discipline the employee.

If you didn't personally observe the behavior, you should have witness statements from people who directly observed the behavior and/or company records that show the employee violated the rule. For example, in a case involving reckless driving of a company vehicle, you should have the police report, witness reports, and a statement from the employee before taking any action.

d. Equal enforcement of the rule

Before imposing discipline, you must check to be sure the rule has been enforced consistently. If there is a company-wide rule, then it has to be enforced consistently throughout the company.

For example, if you only tolerate employees being tardy once a month but other supervisors never say anything about tardiness, then there is unequal enforcement of a company-wide rule. In that case, you will not be able to discipline the employee. However, if you have a job-related departmental safety rule against wearing tennis shoes and it is violated, the only question is whether you have enforced the rule evenly within your department in the past.

e. Progressive Discipline Plus

You also have to show that you made a reasonable effort to change the employee's behavior. You do this by applying progressive discipline plus. In progressive discipline plus, depending on the severity of the problem, you try to change the employee's behavior by first counseling the employee, then training or retraining the employee, then warning and disciplining the employee, and finally terminating the employee. Exhibit 3 shows how progressive discipline plus is designed to work. Different companies use different last step options including suspension with or without pay, final written warning, probation, and/or last chance agreements. You should use the last step option preferred by your company.

Exhibit 3

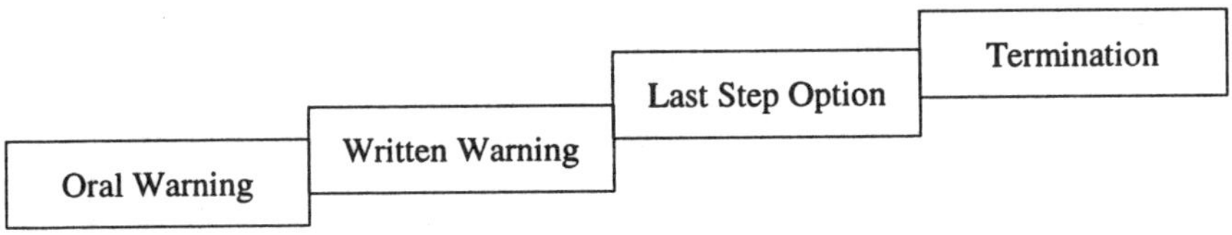

Formal Actions: You must talk with the employee, make notes in your critical incidents diary, and write a memo explaining that you have taken a disciplinary action. The employee must receive a copy of the memo and a copy must be placed in the employee's personnel file.

CONSEQUENCE LINE*

Informal Actions: You must talk to the employee and make a note in your critical incidents diary.

---

*Your goal above and below the consequence line is to create an opportunity for the employee to succeed. The consequence of failure below the line is informal action. The consequence above the line is formal action up to and including termination. When you use the steps above the line, you must tell the employee in writing that his or her job is in jeopardy.

Inability to Perform

An employee's inability to perform the work, or his/her failure in performing the job is the second valid, objective reason for discipline. If you can document a decline in performance or can show that the employee's performance does not meet a reasonable, objective standard, then you have an absolute right to discipline and, if necessary, terminate the employee.

In an inability to perform case, you must show three things:

1. Reasonable standard of performance

An employee cannot be disciplined for failing to meet a standard that was never described. General standards such as "be a good worker" or "do a better job next time" are insufficient standards of performance. The standard must be related to a measurable behavior or the result to be achieved. For example, if you are supervising sales personnel, you might set a behavioral standard like, "You will make three calls a day on old customers and two calls a day on potential new customers," or you might set a results standard, "You will sell $105,000 a month."

Performance standards must be reasonable. You cannot set a standard for an employee that is unreachable, or that other similar employees are not required to meet.

An excellent way to document a performance standard case is to ask the employee at each step of the process to write a memo to you. For example, when you set performance objectives, you can ask the employee to write a memo to you explaining the performance objectives that you expect him or her to meet. In a performance review, ask the employee to write a memo to you describing how she or he has met the performance objectives.

2. Documented failure to meet the objectives

You must show the employee failed to meet the performance standard. Performance cases often fall apart because the company cannot prove failure to meet the performance objective. If you have set a results objective, then you have to produce records to show that the result was not achieved. If you have set a behavioral objective, then you will have to produce documented observations that the employee did not meet the required standard.

3. Progressive discipline plus

If an employee is not performing satisfactorily, it is critical that you give him or her a fair chance to succeed. The best way for you to show that you have given the employee a fair chance to succeed is to use progressive discipline plus. The normal steps in progressive discipline plus are:

Training
Counseling
Oral warning
Written warning
Last step option
Termination

Different companies use different last step options including suspension with or without pay, final written warning, probation, and/or last chance agreements.

Your role as a supervisor is to ensure that you have done everything reasonably possible to help (coach, counsel, train) the employee to succeed and to objectively document the employee's behavior and the actions you have taken.

4
SUMMARY

As a supervisor, it is your responsibility to direct and coach the work of your employees. However, simply directing and coaching employees is not good enough. Today, an effective supervisor must document all significant events with employees. If an employee fails to meet your expectations or fails to follow established company rules, it is your responsibility to carefully and objectively document his or her behavior.

FOSA+ is a five-step system to help you properly document the behavior of your employees. FOSA+ stands for:

FOSA+ Step 1: Facts

Facts are specific observations; not conclusions, assumptions, or probabilities. Facts are objective statements about what you or others saw, heard, touched, smelled, or tasted in relation to employee behavior. Facts include your conversations with the employee plus your prior objectives, prior solutions and prior actions. When written objectively, facts allow the reader to draw the same conclusion that you have drawn in taking a disciplinary action against the employee.

FOSA+ Step 2: Objectives

Objectives describe the behavior you expect the employee to exhibit. They describe what you want the employee to do. Objectives can be written in behavioral terms or results terms.

FOSA+ Step 3: Solutions

Solutions are suggestions to help the employee reach the objectives you have established. Solutions are ideas that you provide to the employee to help him or her succeed in the job. Solutions establish that fact that you are working to help the employee succeed on the job.

FOSA+ Step 4: Action

Action describes the consequences of the employee failing to meet the established objectives. Action is stated in two parts: (1) what step you are taking now; and (2) what step you will take if the employee's behavior does not change. Action warns the employee that if the objectives are not met, you will continue to follow the steps of progressive discipline up to and including termination if the employee does not correct his or her behavior.

When carefully followed, FOSA+ provides documentation that will clearly establish that the employee's behavior is unacceptable and that you have made every effort to help the employee succeed before taking any disciplinary action. FOSA+ is designed to focus attention on the behavior of the employee. Most importantly, FOSA+ documents that you have done your job as a supervisor in dealing with employee problems.

SUMMARY

DISCIPLINE FLOWCHART

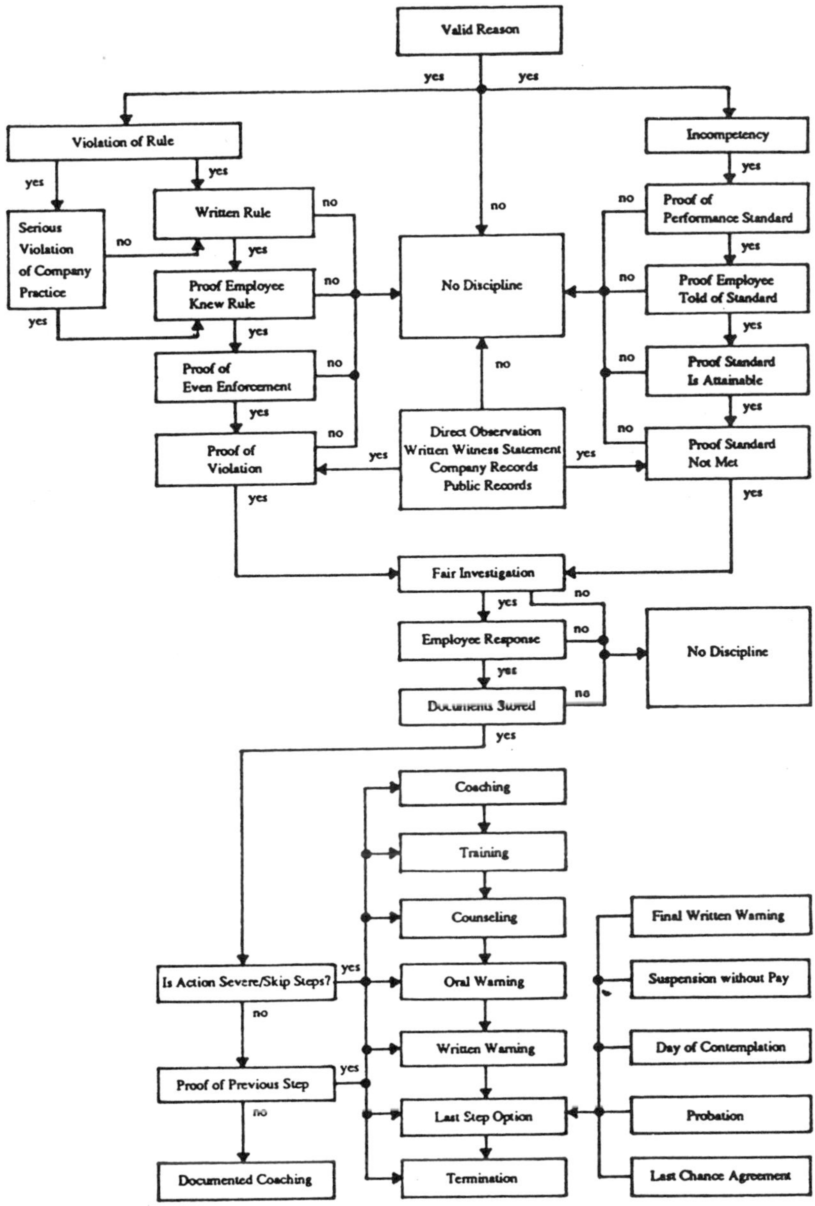

CHECKLIST BEFORE DISCIPLINE

____ Valid Reason for Discipline

- ____ Violation of Rule
  - ____ Rule Exists (____ Written
  - ____ Consistent Practice)
- ____ Employee aware of rule (Proof?)
- ____ Rule Enforced Evenly (Examples)
- ____ Rule Violated (Proof Documented)

____ Incompetency

- ____ Standard of Performance (Explained to employee)
- ____ Standard Reasonable (Can be attained by average employee)
- ____ Standard Not Met (Objective Observations)

____ Fair Investigation (Objective review of events)

____ Progressive Discipline Plus

Documented:

- ____ Coaching ____ Counseling
- ____ Training ____ Oral Warnings

____ Written Warnings (Dates-FOSA)

____ Next-to-Last Step

- ____ Final Written Warning, or,
- ____ Suspension, or
  - ____ without pay
  - ____ with pay
- ____ Probation, or,
- ____ Last Chance Agreement

Documented Supervisory Statement

Facts:

- ____ Employee Behavior
  - ____ Objective Observation
- ____ "Objectified" Statements

____ Prior Supervisory Conversations

- ____ Prior Progressive Discipline Plus

____ Effects of Employee Behavior

- ____ Additional Costs
- ____ Damage Reports

____ Third Party Statements

- ____ Witness Statements
- ____ Official Reports

____ Employee Response

- ____ Employee Statement
- ____ Supervisory Notes
- ____ Silent Witness

Objectives:

- ____ Specific Expected Behavior, or
- ____ Specific Expected Results

Solutions:

- ____ Coaching
- ____ Training
- ____ Resource Personnel
- ____ Resource Materials

Action:

Current:

- ____ Counseling
- ____ Training
- ____ Oral Warning
- ____ Written Warning
- ____ Last Step Option
- ____ Termination

Future:

- ____ Evaluation
- ____ Future Discipline
- ____ Termination

____ Document Retention

- ____ Copies of all documents in a separate secure file

INCIDENT INVESTIGATION REPORT

Date of Incident ____________________

Time of Incident ____________________

Employees Involved:

Description of Incident:

Witnesses: Names   Addresses   Phone

List Documents Attached:

Date of Report: ____________________   Supervisor: ____________________

SAMPLE DOCUMENTATION

TABLE OF FORMS

1. Performance Objectives Memo 37
2. Counseling Memo 41
3. Memorandum of Oral Warning—Poor Work Performance 43
4. Memorandum of Oral Warning—Violation of Work Rule 45
5. Written Warning—Poor Work Performance 47
6. Written Warning—Violation of Work Rule 51
7. Suspension Notice—Poor Work Performance 53
8. Suspension Notice—Violation of Work Rule 57
9. Probation Notice—Poor Work Performance 59
10. Probation Notice—Violation of Work Rule 61
11. Day of Contemplation Memo—Violation of Work Rule 63
12. Last Chance Agreement—Violation of Work Rule 65
13. Termination Notice—Poor Work Performance 67
14. Termination Notice—Violation of Work Rule 69

1. Performance Objectives Memo

November 7, 2005

To: Pat Miller, Personnel Assistant
From: Eric Westbrook, Personnel Manager
Re: Performance Objectives

Your work assignments are an important part of the human resources management services we provide to the company, its employees, and job applicants. In addition to the feedback I have provided in your annual performance review, I am writing this memo to establish specific performance objectives for you to accomplish in the upcoming year. I have divided these objectives into two groups-on-going objectives and specific objectives for the upcoming year.

It is very important that you meet or exceed the following on-going performance objectives:

1. Recruitment Planning: Each recruitment must be carefully planned to ensure that a qualified applicant pool is generated. Planning the recruitment involves developing a written action plan that includes: (a) a review of the company affirmative action plan for the job category that the position is in; (b) a review of applications currently on file to determine if an adequate candidate pool already exists; (c) an advertising campaign that considers the geographic location of potential applicants and effective newspaper and journal advertising; and, (d) a planned testing procedure including paper and pencil tests (where appropriate) and job-related interviews.

2. Recruitment Files: A recruitment file must be established for each recruitment. The file must contain the Personnel Requisition, copies of all advertisements and invoices, all employment applications, and all applicant tracking information. The files must be kept up to date. All filing must be completed before the end of each business day.

3. Relationships With Line Departments: Your job involves working closely with each company department. I expect you to establish effective working relationships with each department. This means that you must be available to departmental representatives to answer questions, provide guidance on recruitment issues and, when necessary, prepare summary reports for supervisors and managers.

In addition to these on-going performance objectives, I expect you to meet the following performance objectives within the next twelve months or by the date indicated below:

1. Turnover Report: You must devise a computer generated report that provides information to analyze employee turnover. The report must be organized by department with a company wide summary. It must include reasons for termination, date of termination, termination costs, and the industry the employee has chosen to work in after leaving our company. The report must be available by the 15th day of each month. Due Date: April 15, 2006 and monthly thereafter.

2. Annual Budget: You must prepare the annual recruiting budget for fiscal year 1993. The budget must include anticipated advertising costs, equipment needs, and travel costs. Each budget item must have a complete narrative description which describes the need for and the expected benefit of the expenditure. Due Date: May 30, 2006.

3. Applicant Flow Analysis: You must continue to prepare a monthly Applicant Flow Analysis. Your report is due by the first working day of each month. It must include a review of the quality and quantity of applicants for each open position. The report must include a cost benefit analysis of each closed recruitment and a projection of anticipated future costs for each open recruitment.

Your position involves considerable public contact. I expect you to conform to the company dress code for public contact positions. I also expect you to utilize the public contact skills you learned in the

"Meeting and Working with the Public" workshop you attended on October 13, 2004. You must keep accurate notes on the progress of each recruitment. Your notes must be handwritten, legible, and filed in the recruitment file. Finally, I expect you to ensure that employment interviews start and end at the scheduled times.

We will discuss these performance objectives on November 18. Please be prepared to ask any questions or express any concerns that you may have regarding these objectives during our meeting. As we move through the year, please feel free to discuss these objectives with me. We will meet monthly to review your progress on each of them as the year progresses.

I have received a copy of this memo:

____________________ ______________

Pat Miller Date

2. Counseling Memo

January 9, 2005

To: Sue McCue, Assembler
From: Danielle Mitchelson, Assembler Supervisor
Re: Counseling Memo

On Friday, January 7, I met with you to discuss your performance as an assembler. I told you at that time that your production rate must improve to 25 parts per hour. You have been averaging 15 parts per hour for the last three weeks. Prior to that time, you averaged 28 parts per hour. On January 7 at 9:20 A.M., I stopped at your work station. Your equipment was not running. The morning plant break is taken at 10:00 A.M. when the whistle blows. You were reading a book. When I asked you why you were reading a book instead of working, you told me that you needed to finish a chapter in your textbook for a night class you are taking.

The average production rate for the other ten assemblers in your unit is 25 parts per hour. When I asked you why you thought your production rate was lower than the other assemblers, you told me that your equipment was not operating properly. I asked the mechanical division to inspect your equipment. They were unable to find any malfunctions in your equipment. Your equipment is the newest in the division. You also told me that you were not comfortable with the new assembly procedures for the Phantom project. When I asked you why you were not comfortable with the project, you told me that it was too complicated for you.

Sue, I know from your past performance that you are capable of meeting the company production standards. However, your performance over the last three weeks is unacceptable. You must improve your average production rate immediately. Your production rate must consistently meet or exceed the 25 parts per hour standard by the end of this month.

Our training department offers a workshop to help assemblers assigned to the Phantom project to improve production efficiency. The next workshop is scheduled for this Thursday. I have signed you up for the workshop. When you attend the workshop, I expect you to pay particular attention to the information related to efficient operation of your equipment. After the workshop, I will discuss the instructional materials with you.

When you are at your work station, you must devote your entire attention to the work which is assigned to you. For safety and productivity reasons, you may not read books or become involved in other nonwork-related activities at your work station.

In order to help you improve your production rate, I am assigning Mary Crosby to assist you for the next two weeks. Mary will instruct you on the proper use of your equipment. She will not do your work for you; however, she will offer suggestions to help you improve your production rate.

The company supports your efforts to further your education. You are receiving benefits from the education reimbursement program. If you need time to study, you should schedule your personal time at home to allow you to complete your reading and homework assignments.

I will meet with you in four weeks to discuss your performance.

I have received a copy of this memo:

____________________ ____________________

Sue McCue Date

3. Memorandum of Oral Warning—Poor Work Performance

February 11, 2005

To: Sue McCue, Assembler
From: Danielle Mitchelson, Assembler Supervisor
Re: Oral Warning

On January 7, I met with you to discuss your work performance. On January 9, I gave you a counseling memo regarding your work performance. On both occasions, I told you that your production rate was averaging 15 parts per hour. I told you that the production rate for your position was an average of 25 parts per hour. I assigned Mary Crosby to work with you for two weeks. I arranged for you to attend a workshop on improving assembler production skills. I told you that it was necessary for you to meet or exceed the average production rate for your position within four weeks.

Your production average for each of the last four weeks has been as follows:

Week Ending	Parts Per Hour
January 16	12
January 23	16
January 30	14
February 7	10

Your overall parts production average for this period is 13 parts per hour. This production level is significantly below the expected average of 25 parts per hour.

This morning, I gave you an oral warning regarding your job performance. I told you that you must improve your per hour parts production average to meet the expected standard immediately. You must average 25 parts per hour for each of the next three weeks.

You can help your production rate by organizing your work area to allow for the efficient movement of work through your station. If you need help, you may ask Mary Crosby to assist you. You attended a workshop on improving your production rate last month. You have your notes and study materials to use to help you operate your equipment efficiently.

If you do not average 25 parts per hour over each of the next three weeks, I will take further disciplinary action. A copy of this Oral Warning will be placed in your personnel file.

I have received a copy of this memorandum of an oral warning.

________________________ ______________________

Sue McCue Date

4. Memorandum of Oral Warning—Violation of Work Rule

February 10, 2004

To: Bruce Black
From: Jim Andreini, Manager
Re: Oral Warning

On December 7, 14, and 21 you were absent from work. Work rule 9 provides: "Employees will be disciplined for excessive absenteeism." Each of these absences was on the day before your scheduled day off. On December 27, I counseled you in regard to your attendance on the job. You were absent on January 5 and 16. On January 29, I counseled you in regard to your attendance on the job and cautioned you that further absences would lead to formal disciplinary action. On February 1, you called in sick. This was the day before your weekend off. When you returned to work February 4, you told Bob Barrett, Supervisor, that you had gone dirt bike riding in the desert. On February 7, 1989, I met with you to discuss your attendance. During this meeting, I gave you an Oral Warning regarding your attendance.

I want to be sure that you understand that I am seriously concerned about your attendance record. I expect you to be at work, on time, every day you are scheduled to work unless you have a bona fide medical emergency which prevents you from coming to work, or are authorized in advance to take time off. If you are unable to come to work you must contact me, Sam Jones, or Jorge Rodriguez in advance. If you do not have advance approval and you do not report to work, you must bring a doctor's note which indicates that you are medically able to return to work before you may begin working.

If you are having medical problems you should use the company medical plan. If you want to take off some of your accumulated vacation, you should submit a request at least two days in advance.

Finally, I told you that unless you follow this directive, you will be subject to further serious disciplinary action.

A copy of this memo of Oral Warning will be placed in your file.

I have received a copy of this memorandum of an oral warning.

__________________________ ____________________

Bruce Black Date

5. Written Warning—Poor Work Performance

May 31, 2005

To: Jose Rodriguez, Sales Executive
From: Nicole Michelle Hartline, Sales Manager
Re: Written Warning-Work Performance

On November 15, I gave you a performance review which addressed your performance for the previous twelve months. Your performance rating for sales accomplishments was "Below Expectations." Your total sales were 40 percent below your established target.

Your overall performance rating was also "Below Expectations." On January 5, I counseled you regarding your continued poor performance in selling company products. Between November 15, 1992 and January 1, you sold $5,000 worth of inventory. Your sales goal for this period was $100,000. During the counseling session, I told you that I expected you to double your contact of prospective customers from 15 per week to 30. I told you that I expected you to meet your sales quota for each week for the next four weeks. I also suggested that you read the company sales manual for additional suggestions on how to better present our products. I made Juanita Brown, Senior Sales Representative, available to you to assist you in organizing your daily work schedule.

On February 10, I gave you an Oral Warning regarding your work performance, specifically, your failure to meet your sales goals. In the four weeks between January 5 and February 5, you sold $10,000 worth of products. Your goal during this period was to sell $20,000 worth of products each week. You failed to meet your sales target by 50 percent. I told you that I expected you to improve your sales rate immediately. I told you that during the period of February 11 through May 15, I expected you to sell at least $100,000 in inventory. I made arrangements to have a mobile telephone put into your car. I also made additional clerical staff available to you to assist you in mailing special sales announcements. In addition, I arranged for you to attend a sales association meeting on February 12 which had several workshops on improving sales volume. I also told you that if you did not meet your sales goals for February 11 through May 15, that you would be subject to disciplinary action up to and including termination.

I have now completed my review of our sales figures from February 11 through May 15. During this period, you sold $30,000. You continue to be significantly behind your established sales goals. When I met with you on May 25 to discuss my preliminary analysis of your sales accomplishments, you told me that you had not met the established quota because your car phone was one week late being installed. You told me that you thought the sales quotas were unreasonable. You told me that you were averaging 18 calls or visits to customers each week. I explained to you that you were the first sales executive in the company to have a mobile telephone and that you were the only salesperson not meeting your sales quotas. Your sales quotas are the same as other sales executives.

I expect you to immediately improve your sales volume. Your sales goal for the next sixty days is $120,000. You must meet this goal. You must increase the number of clients that you telephone or visit each week from your current average of 18 per week to at least 30 per week. Your mobile telephone is now installed and fully operational. I expect you to make use of it in between site visits to make calls to current or potential customers.

The company is offering a time management workshop for sales executives. The next workshop is scheduled for June 10. I suggest that you attend and pay particular attention to the parts of the presentation related to organizing your work to accomplish more work each day. You should ask Theo Jones to help you review your approach to customers to ensure that you are making an effective presentation when you approach them. I will accompany you on three separate sales calls during the next sixty days. I will be with you to observe your performance and to offer suggestions to assist you in being more effective in your sales presentations.

This memo will serve as a written warning regarding your job performance. It will be placed in your personnel file. If you do not meet the sales goal established for you in the next sixty days, I will take further disciplinary action up to and including termination.

I have received a copy of this memorandum.

______________________ ____________________

Jose Rodriguez Date

6. Written Warning—Violation of Work Rule

February 15, 2006

To: Bruce Black
From: Diane Cordray, Manager
Re: Written Warning

On December 27 and on January 29, I counseled you about your attendance and cautioned you that further absences would lead to formal disciplinary action. On February 10, I gave you an Oral Warning regarding your attendance at work. The Oral Warning was based on the fact that you were absent from work on December 7, 14, and 21; January 5 and 16; and February 1. With the exception of January 5, each of these absences was on the day before your days off. I told you that you were expected to be at work by 8:00 A.M. each day you are scheduled to work. I told you that you were expected to be at your work station and ready to begin work at 8:00 A.M. I told you that the only exceptions to this requirement would be if you were medically unable to report to work or if you were scheduled in advance with my approval to take a vacation or personal day off. I also told you that you were required to bring a note signed by a physician for any future absence. I also cautioned you that any additional unexcused absences would lead to further disciplinary action.

Yesterday, February 14, you called in sick. When you returned to work this morning, you had no excuse for your absence. I asked you for a note from a physician that indicated you are medically able to return to work. You told me you did not have a note and that you did not want to get one. Company rule 9 provides: "Repeated unexcused absences or a pattern of unexcused absences is grounds for discipline."

Bruce, I expect you to be at work, on time, every day you are scheduled to work for the next three months unless you have a bona fide medical emergency which prevents you from coming to work or are authorized in advance to take time off. If you must miss work, you must call me directly. If for any reason I am not available, you must speak to Sam Jones or Jorge Rodriguez. If you do miss work, you must bring a physician's note with you upon your return in order to begin working. If you do not bring a note, you will not be permitted to begin working.

Bruce, if you are in need of medical attention, the company has provided a health plan which covers the majority of your costs for treatment after you meet your deductible. I suggest that you take advantage of this benefit to correct any medical problems.

This written warning will be placed in your personnel file. If you do not meet the attendance objectives I have outlined in this memo, you will be subject to further disciplinary action up to and including termination.

I have received a copy of this memorandum.

________________________ ____________________

Bruce Black Date

7. Suspension Notice—Poor Work Performance

July 15, 2005

To: Jane P. Lewis, Fork Lift Driver
From: Steve White, Fork Lift Supervisor
Re: Suspension Notice-Work Performance

On January 12, I gave you a performance review. In it, I told you that your performance was below expectations in the job categories of safety, work production, and equipment maintenance. I established performance objectives for you in each of these job categories.

The objectives were:

1. To operate your fork lift safely and in accordance with the company fork lift operation manual. You were trained in the safe operation of a fork lift on November 12.

2. To complete work assignments on time each day in accordance with the loading schedule for each delivery truck. If you anticipate any problems with completing your daily work assignments, you are to contact me immediately.

3. To maintain your assigned fork lift by checking the oil and water levels each day; by checking all hoses, tires, and mechanical devices for leaks, wear, or other signs of potential malfunction and reporting repair needs to the mechanical division immediately. You are to use the back up forklift if your equipment is not available for any reason.

On February 22, I counseled you regarding your continued failure to meet performance expectations for your position. The counseling session was a result of the fact that you had not completed loading three trucks as assigned on February 21. In the counseling session, I re-explained the performance objectives I had established for you in the performance review. You told me that you understood these objectives and that you would make every effort to meet them.

On March 10, I gave you an Oral Warning regarding your failure to complete your loading assignments for the day. You were assigned to load three trucks. Two of the three trucks were loaded at the end of the day. Your failure to load the third truck resulted in a late shipment to the International Briefcase Company (IBC). IBC rejected the delivery which cost our company $11,325. When I asked you why you had not reported to me that you were behind schedule, you told me that you were tired of being told what to do and that you didn't care if the work was not completed. In the Oral Warning, I told you that it was your responsibility to report to me whenever you would be unable to complete your work assignment. I also told you that if you thought you were behind in your work, you could contact Joe Smith, Lead Fork Lift Operator, for assistance.

On May 25, I gave you a Written Warning concerning your work performance. On May 23, you did not complete your assigned work. You were assigned to load four trucks during the day. You were also assigned to work 3 hours overtime. All three fork lift drivers were assigned to load four trucks on May 25. You were the only operator who did not to complete his or her work assignments. The loads and trucks were identical for all fork lift operators.

At the morning break, I asked you if you were on schedule. You told me, "No problem boss man." During the day, you did not report to me or to Joe Smith that you were behind in your loading schedule. Joe Smith, Lead Fork Lift Operator, reported to me that you were driving your fork lift over the longest possible route between picking up loads throughout the day. When I asked you why you were doing this, you told me that you were tired of seeing the same part of the warehouse each day. I told you that you were to drive from the loading dock directly to the load and back to the truck throughout the day. I also told you that if you had any questions regarding the route you are to drive that you should ask Joe Smith immediately.

On July 13, you did not complete your assigned work schedule.

You were assigned to load three trucks on that day. The other Fork Lift Operators were assigned to load five trucks on July 13. Your assigned work was less than the other operators because I have been unable to depend on you to complete your loads and the July 13 shipment was critical. You did not report to me or to Joe Smith that you were behind in your work. When I asked you at noon if you were on schedule you told me, "You'll have nothing to worry about boss." At 4:00 P.M., I asked you if you were still on schedule to be completed by 5:00 P.M. You told me that it would be impossible for you to get everything done. You told me that one of your tires was low on air but that you did not want to use the back up fork lift because it was older than the one you are used to driving.

I have instructed you to report to me or to Joe Smith whenever you think you will be late with your work assignment. I have also told you that it is your responsibility to check your equipment daily and that you are to use the back up fork lift if there are any mechanical problems with your assigned equipment.

You failed to complete your assigned work on February 21, March 10, May 23, and July 13. I have discussed the importance of completing your work with you during your performance review in January; in a counseling session on February 22; in an Oral Warning on March 10, and; in a Written Warning on May 25. On each of these occasions, I told you that you were to contact either myself or Joe Smith if you were behind schedule. I have also instructed you to check your equipment daily and to use the back up fork lift if your assigned equipment had any mechanical problems. You have not met the performance objectives which have been set for you despite my attempts to assist you in understanding your work assignments.

As a result of your continued failure to meet your assigned performance objectives, I am placing you on a three (3) day suspension without pay. During this suspension, I expect you to carefully consider your job responsibilities. I expect you to meet the performance objectives for your position. If you do not meet these objectives, you will be subject to termination. A copy of this memo will be placed in your personnel file.

I have received a copy of this memorandum.

____________________________ ____________________________

Jane P. Lewis Date

8. Suspension Notice—Violation of Work Rule

February 29, 2005

To: Irving Schultz-Warehouse Worker
From: Ron Vasquez-Warehouse Manager
Re: Suspension Notice

On December 27, I warned you about your conduct at the company holiday party. I told you that the company has a strict written rule against sexual jokes between employees and that the company does not permit any form of sexual harassment. I reminded you that you have attended two harassment prevention seminars including one put on by the company three months ago. At the party I Heard you tell an inappropriate gender based joke. I told you at that time that any future violations of this rule would result in severe discipline.

On February 24, you worked late with Sylvia Porter. The next morning she reported that you told her three sexual jokes. She told me that when she asked you to stop, you told her to "lighten up." After conducting an investigation, I asked you for your version. You at first denied that any incident had occurred and suggested she was out to get you. When I told you other employees had heard the jokes, you admitted that you had been telling jokes.

You are directed to follow the company's sexual harassment policy, a copy of which is attached. Sexual harassment includes matters that you may think are not harassing but which are offensive to the recipient. You must avoid making any comments or telling any jokes that are gender or sexual in nature when you are on company property or at company related functions.

In the event that you have questions about what conduct is appropriate, I suggest that you see me before engaging in it.

Your actions are in violation of strict company rules. In addition they are abusive to employees and destructive of morale. Because of your repeated violations of this same company rule and your lack of candor in the investigation of this matter, I am suspending you without pay from February 15 through February 20. If you engage in any further violations of this rule you will be terminated immediately.

I have received a copy of this memo:

____________________	______________
Irving Schultz	Date

9. Probation Notice—Poor Work Performance

July 6, 2005

To: Ralph Jones, Vice President of Sales
From: Kent Risly, President
Re: Performance Objectives

On January 5, we discussed the poor performance in the sales department for the 2004 year. I told you at that time our sales would have to increase substantially in the near future if we were going to remain a major force in our market. I also told you that based on our market research the problem was not the product but the fact that our sales representatives were being outsold by the competition. Eighty-five percent of our lost sales orders last year were due to poor follow-up by our sales force including not returning phone calls, missing deadlines, and incorrect sales orders.

On January 5, we agreed on your performance objectives in the sales department for the 2005 year and set an annual target of $240 million in sales and a monthly target of $20 million. The sales figures for the first six months of this year stand at $100 million or a rate of $16,666,666 a month. This is a reduction from last year of $1,833,700 per month (a 9.9 percent decline) and is 16 percent below the goal that we set.

Last Tuesday, when I met with you to discuss these figures you told me that you had implemented several new programs and did not understand why they were not working. You asked me for more time to make the program work.

The current level of sales in this company is unacceptable. Sales orders for the last six months of this calendar year must average $20 million per month. In addition, total sales for the last six months of this year must be at least $110 million.

You are authorized to bring in our outside sales consultant to help you with this turnaround. In addition, I will be available to help you at your request.

This next six months is a probationary period for you. If you do not meet the goals outlined above you will be terminated.

I have received a copy of this notice:

__________________________ __________________________

Ralph Jones Date

10. Probation Notice—Violation of Work Rule

March 1, 2004

To: Bruce Black
From: Diane Cordray, Supervisor
Re: Notice of Disciplinary Probation

During the last three months, you have been absent on the following dates:

Month	Date	Reason
December	7	None
	14	None
	21	None
January	5	None
	16	None
February	1	Dirt Bike Riding
	14	Physician Note
April	27	Surfing

You were cautioned that your actions would lead to further disciplinary action on the following dates:

Month	Date	Action
December	27	Counseling
January	29	Counseling
February	10	Oral Warning
February	15	Written Warning

On February 25, you called in sick. You spoke to Sam Spade, Plant Manager. You told him you had a headache. You returned to work on February 26, without a note from a physician. You were sent home to get a physician's note. You returned to work with a note on February 27.

The company has strict rules on employee attendance. The employee handbook provides "Excessive absence is grounds for discipline."

You have been repeatedly cautioned to improve your attendance record. Your absence rate is 75 percent higher than any other employee in this department. There does not appear to be any legitimate reason for your absences.

You must be at work on time every work day. If miss work, you must either have my permission in advance or have a serious and unforeseeable emergency. In the event you are absent without my permission you will be required to document that your absence was due to a serious and unforeseeable emergency.

You may wish to seek assistance from the company's employee assistance program counselors. They have successfully assisted other employees who have had absentee and tardiness problems. Their telephone number is (714) 555-0903.

I am placing you on disciplinary probation for the next ninety days. If you miss any work time for other than a serious, proven emergency during this time you will be terminated.

I have received a copy of this memorandum.

______________________ ______________________

Bruce Black Date

11. Day of Contemplation Memo—Violation of Work Rule

March 28, 2004

To: Alice Bear
From: Sonia Trustheart, Manager
Re: Day of Contemplation

On March 24, I instructed you to change work locations and to work in the Accounting Department until there was more work to perform in Auditing. You informed me that you did not like the people in Accounting and did not want to work with "bean counters." I explained to you that because our computer was down we were temporarily overstaffed in Auditing and that the move was only temporary. You said you would go, but would not like it.

This is the third time an incident of this sort has occurred. On December 12, I directed you to help on the Warehouse inventory and you stated that you did not like to work with "sweaty no-necks." At that time I told you that this is a company that works together and that your refusal to work with other people was not in keeping with our practices.

On February 4, while I was out of town I left a message for you to work with the Accounting department on the annual report. When I returned I found that you had neither contacted Accounting or done any work with them on the annual report. When I asked you why you had not worked with them you stated that it was too demeaning. The Employee Handbook rule 3 provides that insubordination or failure to follow instructions of a supervisor is grounds for discipline. I gave you a written letter of reprimand for not following orders.

You are directed not to report to work on March 29. You will be paid for the day.

On March 30, you are directed to report to work with a written memo directed to me in which you state the behavioral problems that we have discussed and how you will change your behavior in regards to working with other departments in this Company. If you have difficulty writing this memo, you may call me at the office on March 29 to discuss the memo.

I will meet with you when you arrive at work on March 30 to review this memo with you. At that time we will agree on a set of performance objectives in regard to your work with other departments in the Company.

I have read and received this memorandum.

________________________	____________________
Alice Bear	Date

12. Last Chance Agreement—Violation of Work Rule

May 22, 1998

To: Bobby Beltron, Mechanic
From: Sam Spade, Supervisor
Re: Last Chance Agreement

In the past six months, you have been absent from work a total of 120 hours. Your supervisor counseled you on January 3 and again on February 1. You received an Oral Warning on March 5, and a Written Warning on March 25. On April 10, you were given three days time off without pay.

The day before yesterday when I called you into my office to tell you that I was strongly considering terminating you and to ask you if there was anything I should know about why you were continuing to be off work, you told me that you have a substance abuse problem that you want to work out. I referred you to our Employee Assistance Program.

Yesterday, you told me that the Employee Assistance Program had recommended that you enter a detoxification program immediately. You have asked me for a 45 day unpaid leave of absence. Your use of controlled substances (drugs) during working hours and on Company premises is a serious violation of Company rules and safety practices which would ordinarily subject you to termination by the Company. Under the circumstances that you have offered to take a drug test and to remain drug free, the Company is prepared to continue employment under the following conditions:

1. You will not possess, use, sell, or be under the influence of any nonprescribed controlled substance on Company premises or on Company time at any time in the future.

2. If you use, or are under the influence of any prescribed substance, you will inform your supervisor of that fact and the nature of the substance that you are taking prior to starting work.

3. You agree that you may be tested for the presence of controlled substances in your system at any time for any reason or for no reason at all during the next two years by a medical testing facility using any appropriate testing procedure. If you are ordered to take such an examination and refuse or fail to take the examination you agree that you will be terminated. If you take the examination and test positive for the presence of controlled substances which you previously had not revealed to your supervisor, you agree that you will be terminated.

In accepting the terms of this Last Chance Agreement, you are agreeing that if you fail to live up to this agreement, you will either immediately resign your position or you will be terminated. No excuses will be accepted for not meeting the terms of this Agreement.

________________________ ________________

[Supervisor] Date

I have read and been given a copy of this Last Chance Agreement. I have been informed that I should review this Agreement with an attorney, a union representative, or any other representative of my choice before I sign it. I understand that this is my last chance to keep my job and that if I violate this Agreement I will be terminated.

________________________ ________________

[Employee] Date

13. Termination Notice—Poor Work Performance

March 21, 2006

To: Jennifer Jones, Driver
From: Robin Freude, Manager
Re: Termination Notice

On January 12, I met with you to discuss customer complaints on your delivery route. I told you that several customers had called in that morning to complain that you had not shown up with their deliveries. I cautioned you that our business requires prompt and courteous deliveries or our customers will use competitors.

On February 2, Glenn Mills called and asked that you not make deliveries to them anymore because you were always late and were rude when they asked you why you were late. At that time you were given a written warning notice and your route was adjusted so that you would not deliver to Glenn Mills.

On March 16, Chase Mills called to say that you had parked your truck in their driveway for an hour blocking all traffic. When they went to look for you on the premises they were unable to find you. When you did arrive, you cursed out their dock manager and left. You were given a three day suspension and told at that time that any future violations would result in immediate termination.

On March 28, you left at the normal time on your route. By 10:00 A.M., we had calls from five customers that you had not shown up to make your normal delivery. When Sam Jones went out looking for you he found your truck at 11:15 A.M., parked in front of a coffee shop on Third and Western. He found you inside. You told him you were taking your coffee break. You have been instructed to take your coffee break as close to 10:00 A.M. as possible. According to your route schedule you were an hour and a half behind in your deliveries. When I asked you why you were late that morning you told me that you had a bigger than usual order at Frampton. I checked that order sheet (attached). It shows a normal Frampton order. I called the dockmaster at Frampton. He stated that he logged your truck in at 9:10 and out at 9:25. A copy of that log sheet is attached.

Based upon your continued poor performance, you are terminated immediately.

I have received a copy of this notice.

________________________ ________________________

Jennifer Jones Date

14. Termination Notice—Violation of Work Rule

April 30, 2006

To: Bruce Black
From: Sam Spade, Plant Manager
Re: Notice of Termination

On December 27, and again on January 29, your supervisor, Diane Cordray, counseled you in regard to your attendance on the job. She reminded you of Work rule 9 "Excessive absenteeism is grounds for discipline." On February 10, Ms. Cordray gave you an Oral Warning regarding your attendance on the job. On February 15, Ms. Cordray gave you a Written Warning regarding your attendance on the job. On March 1, you were placed on disciplinary probation and told that if you were absent from work for any reason other than a bona fide medical emergency for three months, you would be subject to termination.

On April 27, you did not report to work. You did not call in and talk to Diane Cordray, Jorge Rodriguez, or me. When you came to work on April 28, you told Ms. Cordray that you had gone to the beach. You did not bring a note from a physician indicating that you had been sick.

I met with you yesterday afternoon to discuss your attendance record and your failure to respond to the numerous warnings issued by Ms. Cordray. You acknowledged that the warnings had been issued and told me that you had gone to the beach on April 28 and that you were not sick on that day.

As a result of your failure to correct your on the job attendance and your failure to respond to numerous oral and written warnings, I am terminating your employment effective immediately.

I have received a copy of this memorandum.

________________________ ________________________

Bruce Black Date

INDEX

References are to page numbers

Communication, 1, 18
Consequence line, 26
Counseling, 3, 5, 21, 26
Critical incidents diary, 3, 6, 24, 26

Documented failure to meet the objectives, 27

Effective documentation, 2, 9
Employee behavior, 2, 9, 10, 25, 29
Employee interview, 13
Equal enforcement of the rule, 24

Formal actions, 26
FOSA+ STEP 1: FACTS, 9, 29
FOSA+ STEP 2: OBJECTIVES, 16, 29
FOSA+ STEP 3: SOLUTIONS, 19, 30
FOSA+ STEP 4: ACTION, 20, 30

Inability to perform, 26
Informal actions, 26
Investigations, 5

Keeping documentation, 6

Last step option, 6, 21, 25, 26, 28
Layoff, 23

Objectivity, 2
Oral warning, 6, 21, 26

Performance objectives, 5
Positive performance, 5
Progressive discipline, 6, 30
Progressive discipline plus, 25, 27
Proof employee knew the rule, 24
Proven violation of the rule, 24

Reasonable standard of performance, 27
Reduction in force, 23
Resource materials, 20
Resource persons, 20

Specific behavior, 17
Specific result, 17

Termination, 2, 6, 21, 26
Third party observations, 12
Training, 5, 19, 27

Violation of company rules, 23